LEEDS COLLEGE OF BUILDING LIBRARY
CLASS NO
BARCODE

KT-450-091

VITAL 3

Effective Leadership in Schools

Book 1

Sharing the vision...

and the distribution of effective leadership

LEEDS COLLEGE OF BUILDING
WITHDRAWN FROM STOCK

Tony Swainston

with Mike Hughes and Adrian Raynor

Published by Network Educational Press Ltd
PO Box 635
Stafford
ST16 1BF

First published 2005
© Tony Swainston 2005

ISBN 1 85539 120 1

The right of Tony Swainston to be identified as the author of this work has been asserted in accordance with Sections 77 and 78 of the Copyright, Designs and Patents Act 1988.

All rights reserved. No part of this publication may be reproduced, stored in a retrieval system or reproduced or transmitted in any form or by any means, electronic, mechanical, photocopying, recording or otherwise, without the prior written permission of the publishers. This book may not be lent, resold, hired out or otherwise disposed of by way of trade in any form of binding or cover other than that in which it is published without the prior consent of the publishers.

Every effort has been made to contact copyright holders of materials reproduced in this book. The publishers apologize for any omissions and will be pleased to rectify them at the earliest opportunity.

Project editor: Anne Oppenheimer
Design and layout: Marc Maynard, Network Educational Press Ltd
Illustrations: Paul Keen and Tony Swainston

Printed in Great Britain by
MPG Books Ltd, Bodmin, Cornwall

Contents

Book 1: Sharing the Vision ... and the distribution of effective leadership

'We shall not cease
from exploration.

And the end of all
our exploring

Will be to arrive
where we started

And know the place
for the first time.'

T. S. Eliot

Introduction

'Vision' and 'distributed leadership'. These twin notions, ideas or concepts in leadership theory have been much talked about in recent years, but they are definitely not new ideas. What we call things may change, but if they have sustainability in terms of effectiveness then we can be confident that they have always been around in one form or another. However, I would argue that neither because these things have already been well discussed, nor because they are happening in certain situations, should we hesitate to look at them in more detail. My reasoning for this is as follows.

1. Unless we are thoroughly aware of what these ideas mean, we can enter into a dark cave when we share thoughts, ideas and views without being fully informed about the things we are talking about. A friend of mine describes this as a discussion which results in a 'pooling of ignorance'. At a DfES research conference in London on 5 December 2003 Andreas Schleicher, head of the OECD Analysis Division, talking about the value of the PISA findings, said 'Without data, you are just another person with an opinion.' In terms of leadership, as in so many aspects of education, we are in need of data which can come from educational research, with which to compare our own 'internal data' or beliefs so that we can then challenge and refine them. Leaders in education must be prepared to use research, either by engaging in it themselves (action research) or by adapting education research findings to their own setting. In this way they present models to the profession of learning and enquiry that are critical for advancement. We may at the end of it all arrive at a position that confirms what we initially thought – but at least then we can feel assured that we are in a stronger position to hold this view. I have used this quote many times before and in my other VITAL books, but for me it has real beauty and power and it is nowhere more relevant than in education itself:

> *We shall not cease from exploration. And the end of all our exploring will be to arrive where we began and to know the place for the first time. (T. S. Eliot)*

2. We should be moving towards a common language in education where we all fully understand what each other is talking about. Again, this is linked to Point 1 above. Without a common language in which we are fairly certain that someone else's words have the same meaning for them as they do for us, we will once again be thrashing in a whirlpool of confusion that prevents progress. A classic example of this at the moment involves the twin notions of 'mentoring' and 'coaching'. It is generally accepted that both mentoring and coaching have a big impact on people involved in these activities. If this is the case, we should all be aware of what these things involve and the distinction between them. Otherwise, what one person calls 'mentoring' another could be thinking of as 'coaching'. Some would argue that this is of no consequence and that as long as you are doing something that works, what you call it is irrelevant. This is simply not true, and it is sheer laziness to think so. It is also a real danger for anyone to think this in education. What every one of us in education should be doing is moving

towards a situation where we can all share our knowledge and understanding. We need to become 'consciously competent' about what we do so that we can advance ourselves, while at the same time being able to share our skills and knowledge with others around us.

3. I mentioned above that there are excellent examples of people with tremendous leadership visions and an excellent working knowledge of distributed leadership. This is true, and I believe that you will witness this through the leaders who are filmed here for VITAL 3. Where there is a clear vision and effective distributed leadership, the impact is truly powerful. However, we must not believe that these things are happening everywhere in education, and we can ourselves assist the situation by reflecting on the essence of them and arriving at a position where we can then influence others in terms of spreading the ideas.

Part 1 will hopefully bring some clarity to why a vision can be so powerful for a leader. It will indicate how a vision can help to move us from a position of being efficient to being effective, and how a vision can stir strong emotions in people that result in an impact on their hearts and minds. In addition, we will look at why distributed leadership is so critical to the development of an education system that can continually develop and improve. Making use of everyone's inner strengths and talents in terms of leadership could take us to a place in education that we can only dream of at the moment.

I hope that you enjoy and find reward in studying Book 1, and that it provides a mechanism for you to reflect by yourself or with colleagues about some of the critical issues impacting on leadership in education today.

Tony Swainston
January 2005

*'For some,
vision is that perfect
state that might
never be reached,
but which one
never stops trying
to achieve.'*

J.R. Latham

Sharing the vision

This section concerns the following:

1.1.1 The passion of a shared vision

> ▸ Is it strong enough to die for?

1.1.2 Taking risks

> ▸ With nothing ventured, there is nothing to be sustained

1.1.3 Effectiveness and efficiency

> ▸ Distinguishing between leadership and management

1.1.4 The leader as a storyteller with beliefs

> ▸ How the story reveals the leader's beliefs

1.1.5 Broad meanings of vision

> ▸ The journey is worth taking for all of us

1.1.6 Finally, this section looks at the responses of the leaders to the questions on vision, which include:

Questions on vision
a) What vision have you for your school?   b) What vision have you for schools in general in the future?   c) How did you create the vision you have for your school?   d) Did you involve other people in creating the vision?   e) How often do you revisit the vision for the school?

1.1.1 The passion of a shared vision

In his book *The Fifth Discipline*, Senge (1990) uses the example of a scene in the film *Spartacus* to demonstrate the idea of passion associated with a shared vision. Spartacus is a Roman gladiator and slave who leads an army of slaves fighting for their freedom in an uprising in 71 BC. Through a united vision, and the associated passion this generated, Spartacus' army managed to defeat the Roman legions twice before being finally defeated by the general Marcus Crassus. The slaves who had survived the battle (about 1,000) were given the chance to be spared their lives, but at the same time to remain as slaves, if they were prepared to turn Spartacus over to Crassus. In true Hollywood fashion, at this moment Spartacus (played by Kirk Douglas) stands up and proclaims, '*I* am Spartacus.' Immediately after this, another slave stands up and says, 'I am Spartacus,' followed by another who says, 'No, *I* am Spartacus,' and so on, until each member of the army of slaves is on his feet.

'Follow the leader!' Most will, without fear, follow a leader who has a clear vision.

A great cinematic moment indeed, but also a useful way of illustrating the power behind a shared vision. All the slaves knew that by standing up in this way that they would die, but to them this was preferable to returning to a life of slavery. The vision they all bought into, the vision that they could be free men, was strong enough to drive them on with passion.

I am reminded here of the often spoken Bill Shankly quote. Bill was the manager of Liverpool Football Club during some of its most romantic and successful seasons. It was impossible, when listening to Bill, not to be impressed by the passion and vision he had for football, and he managed to get footballers to achieve standards that they themselves probably didn't believe they could achieve. Bill's famous comment about football was:

LEEDS COLLEGE OF BUILDING LIBRARY

> *Some people think that football is a matter of life and death... I can assure them it is much more serious than that.*

Like Spartacus, Bill Shankly lived and breathed what he talked about, and people around him were inspired and bought into his vision. Every member of Liverpool FC at that time seemed to be empowered by a shared vision. Senge (1990) goes on to describe the notion of a shared vision as follows:

> 'A shared vision is not an idea. It is not even an important idea such as freedom. It is, rather, a force in people's hearts, a force of impressive power. It may be inspired by an idea, but once it goes further – if it is compelling enough to acquire the support of more than one person – then it is no longer an abstraction. It is palpable. People begin to see it as if it exists. Few, if any, forces in human affairs are as powerful as a shared vision.'

In organizations, imagine the almost unstoppable force that would be created if everyone could support a certain vision. The skill of the leader is to be able to generate the support for the vision through a common caring. A vision that is shared will then connect with people's own individual aspirations, which then combine for the collective good. Senge also talks about the way in which a 'shared vision fosters risk-taking and experimentation'. In schools of today and tomorrow this is absolutely essential if the education system is to move forward and provide greater coherence coupled with personalized learning for each individual.

1.1.2 Taking risks

We certainly don't know all the answers and we never will, but to seek out, to experiment, to take risks, to be allowed to fail and learn from the failures as much as from successes, is essential if we are to learn and develop. This is a core element for the learning school, something that is now talked about by many people, and a shared vision can make this a reality. In a shared vision each individual will have their own perspective, and their own individual and particular contribution to make. Each of these contributions combines within the collective whole, making the collective stronger than any of the individual elements. One missing part will not let the whole fall apart. Perhaps this is a useful way of approaching the idea of capacity building, which is something that is talked about a lot – though often, it would appear, with little understanding about what it really entails. It might be argued that the progress towards capacity building for any school could be enhanced through a shared vision which will provide the general feel, structure, ethos and passion within the organization to constantly assist its growth.

Achieving a shared vision cannot be done simply by sitting down and experiencing one of those inspirational personal moments where everything seems clear. (Not that I have personally experienced many of these in any case!) In fact, there is a lot of unglamorous work that needs to be done for a vision to become something that is shared by everybody. It often involves going about the everyday business while always keeping the vision in mind. It also requires a high level of listening and being in tune with the general messages that the organization is bringing forth. Senge (1990) says:

'The hallmark of a learning organization is not lovely visions floating in space, but a relentless willingness to examine "what is" in the light of our vision.'

Many schools have tried to come up with a vision based on a short period of concentrated discussions and dissemination, but Senge (2003) warns that:

'... it is highly unlikely that a brief process, such as a two-day retreat and a two-hour assembly, can lead to a true shared vision.'

Reaching a shared vision requires time and commitment. Smith and Lucas (in Senge 2003) say that the shared vision design has three separate but related purposes. These are illustrated diagrammatically below.

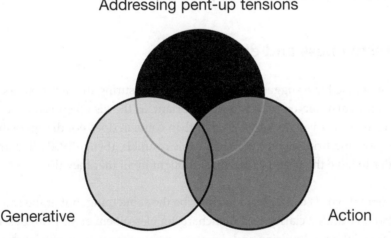

- ▸ **Addressing pent-up tensions**: people, both individually and collectively, need to be able to give voice to their problems. This requires a degree of courage in schools to allow the difficulties that people face to be opened up for discussion.

- ▸ **Generative**: people must be given the opportunity to speak about their greatest hopes and desires for the pupils, school community and broader community. It is important not simply to linger on the problems but also to discuss the real possibilities. From this, I would argue, come the imagination and creativity that can invigorate and replenish the drive that may otherwise lie dormant in the school.

▸ **Action**: people must be given the opportunity to be responsible for creating the future of the school and to work collectively in doing this. This requires a level of distributed leadership, which I shall discuss in Chapter 2, and comprises one of the questions we ask the leaders for VITAL 3. Some people will perceive great risk associated with this strategy, but the rewards are immense.

All of this does not to diminish, but rather complements, the role of the leader in being able to describe what the vision is. This is very important in terms of giving credibility and strength to the message. Bass (1985; and in Kakabadse et al. 1998), for example, postulates that, besides other qualities, transformational leaders require an ability to articulate their vision. The leader of a school does this in a variety of ways which are visible, such as assemblies, staff meetings, governors' meetings, meetings with parents and so on, as well as the more subtle ways which involve private discussions with teachers, support staff and all the personnel that combine to make the workforce in the school. Other writers, such as Nanus (in Kakabadse et al. 1998), also emphasize the importance of what the leader does on a day-to-day basis. He says, 'for visions to be effective, leaders have to live the vision by making all their actions and behaviours consistent with it, and by creating a sense of urgency and passion for attainment.' A school leader can be a good communicator through the art of oratory, but this must be within a firm framework of integrity and moral purpose if the message is to have a sustainable impact.

Hunt (1991) talks about the need for exemplary behaviour, personally communicating the vision, demonstrating trustworthiness, displaying respect and taking risks, as a necessary requirement for turning a vision into reality. What is interesting for me here is that Hunt, like Senge, links risk-taking with a shared vision.

1.1.3 Effectiveness and efficiency

A number of people have suggested that one way of ensuring that a vision doesn't fail is to provide some early successes. It is also important, as the vision spreads and involves more people, that the diversity of views that then come in does not dissipate the clarity of central vision and bring about 'unmanageable conflicts' (Senge 1990). It is important for the leader to have the vision as a central thought in all that they do.

At times different words can be used to describe the same thing, but at the same time they can also give added clarity. Ken Blanchard)in Hesselbein et al. 1996) describes how effectiveness is linked with vision and direction in the same way as efficiency is associated with systems and procedures. He says:

'When people talk about effectiveness, they are basically talking about vision and direction. Effectiveness has to do with focusing the organization's energy in a particular direction. When people talk about efficiency, they are talking about systems and procedures – the way things are done.'

This also perhaps helps to highlight the distinction between leadership and management. The diagram below may help to illustrate this.

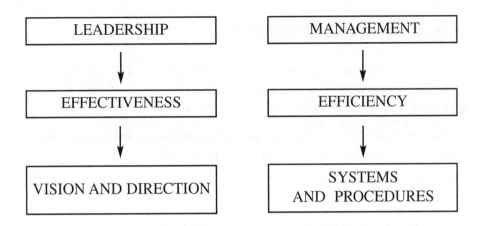

Management, efficiency, systems and procedures are all important, but without leadership, effectiveness, vision and direction it might well be that all the effort expended could be in the wrong direction. Stephen Covey's ideas on this are referred to on page 21 of *Effective Teachers* (Swainston 2000), and it would be useful to refer to this at some stage.

1.1.4 The leader as a storyteller with beliefs

The importance of the 'stories' that a leader communicates to others is emphasised by Sergiovanni (2002). The stories that a leader tells and demonstrates through actions are a way of living out the vision. Sergiovanni says:

'If the leader is effective, then her or his stories become the school's stories, providing the sense of identity and coherence that holds things together as the school struggles to make its stories a reality.'

The concept of the storyteller-leader is an interesting one, and to my mind the story is told by the everyday movements that a leader makes, the actions that tell the reality of what is going on internally, as well as the words that are spoken. In fact, as Sergiovanni argues, leadership is about more than merely using words to state specific objectives, then developing strategies, and getting measurable results. Beliefs are vitally important in all of this – and beliefs, tied to visions, are perhaps viewed as soft quantities, and as a result hard to measure, but they are critically important. Beliefs are what help to shape us as human beings. John Gardner (in Sergiovanni 2002) says:

'Humans are believing animals. They have religious beliefs. They hold to one or another political doctrine. They have beliefs that supply meaning in lives, beliefs that tell them how to conduct themselves, beliefs that console. The leader that understands those beliefs and acts in terms of that understanding has tapped a source of power.'

Trying to access, assess and, at times, to shape and modify people's belief systems is an essential role of a leader and should form part of their vision.

1.1.5 Broad meanings of vision

In an attempt to define vision still further, Reeves, McCall and MacGilchrist (in MacBeath and Mortimore 2001) give a useful summary of the three broad meanings attributed to the word 'vision' in the literature. These are:

▸ a common goal which can be embodied in a simple statement that serves to unite everyone – **A COMMON AND SHARED PURPOSE**

▸ the ability of leaders to take a holistic view of the organization – **THE CURRENT REALITY**

▸ the ability of the organization, through its leaders, to see where it is going – **HAVING A SENSE OF DIRECTION**.

We have already looked at the common shared purpose or shared vision. In addition, having a sense of direction is probably part of what people generally think of as an element in a vision. What perhaps is of most interest here is the importance of a leader's acquiring a clear picture of the current reality. Understanding not only the present circumstances of the organization but also the *reason* for the present circumstances is critically important if the organization is to be able to move forward.

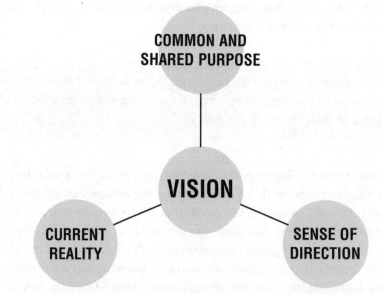

Kakabadse et al. (1998) supports these notions of vision being an understanding of the present position and where the organization should go, and says:

> 'Vision constitutes partly the sensing, by an individual, of what an organization or system should look like and/or how it works, and partly how this working organization is to be taken into the future. As such, visions are based on a web of beliefs, both supported and mediated by each individual's personal values and beliefs.'

Kakabadse expands on this by saying that a vision is about 'possibilities, desired futures, and an expression of optimism and hope'. Another important aspect to mention here is the importance of the journey that is taken as a consequence of a vision. The journey can be as important as the final destination – in fact, the final destination may never be reached. This brings in another view of what vision is all about. The drive, the desire, the optimism and the hope embodied in a vision all create a momentum that can be steered towards the perceived final outcome.

> *For some, vision is that perfect state that might never be reached, but which one never stops trying to achieve. (Latham, in Kakabadse et al. 1998)*

Although the final state may never be found, nevertheless, with a clear vision, sharply in focus, a leader can make great strides in the right direction along the intended road.

> *Vision constitutes partly the sensing, by an individual, of what an organization or system should look like and/or how it works, and partly how this working organization is to be taken into the future. As such, visions are based on a web of beliefs, both supported and mediated by each individual's personal values and beliefs. (Kakabadse et al. 1998)*

With a clear vision the journey can prove to be as important as the destination.

1.1.6 Vision – what the leaders filmed for VITAL 3 say

Let's turn now to what the leaders in VITAL 3 say about vision.

Referring to the question 'What vision have you for your school?' on the DVD we hear David refer to the need to *'live the vision'* and say that he doesn't think it is essential to have a written statement of the vision.

Derek also talks about living the vision every day, and how the vision for the school is constantly revisited with both new and established staff. Derek gives a good example of how the school lives out its passion for the vision of excellence in teaching and learning through the active reflection that takes place each Wednesday, when the pupils leave the school early at 2pm, giving the staff time to talk about the important issues connected with teaching and learning, among other things. This reinforces the views expressed above that the *actions* taken within an organization give a far clearer picture of the vision that exists than a vision statement that is written down. This is not to discard the usefulness of a written vision statement in certain contexts and for certain organizations, (particularly if it is the result of a formative thought process), but only to say that by itself, it does not provide a great deal of substance.

David's vision for the school is about providing a sense of belonging as a result of people being welcomed, and as a result people performing to a high standard.

Anne's vision includes being at the forefront of educational initiatives with the spin-offs this provides of working with other schools, further education institutions, higher education institutions and others. This style of vision, Anne believes, helps to ensure that the school moves forward.

Phil reflects on his experience as a headteacher and feels that in the past headteachers were more idiosyncratic than they are today, with vision not necessarily being part of their everyday thought process. However, through structured programmes such as the NPQH (National Professional Qualification for Headteachers), the importance of a vision is now more recognized by present and up-and-coming headteachers. Theresa talks about the work she has carried out on teaching and learning with the teachers in her school. A commitment to every child being given an individual entitlement is something that is part of Theresa's vision, and matches well the current concentration on personalized learning.

Mike reflects honestly on how a leader's own idea of the school vision may not always coincide with the perceptions of every member of the school. He describes how he carries out checks to ensure that the vision is one that is ultimately shared within the school.

Janet describes an exciting and challenging atmosphere in the school as part of her vision, while Helen expresses a desire to see all members of her community fulfilling their potential as a major part of hers. Susan refers to a caring school with the logo *'Quality has no finish line'*– which echoes the notion mentioned earlier, that the vision may never be finally attained.

Taking a walk outside the school can bring great rewards.

Iain says that *'excellence becoming a habit'* is part of his vision for the school, and Kay talks about the vision of the school as very much a shared one which is invoked every time the school plans are reviewed. Derek talks about a school with a safe, secure, supportive environment in which the best teaching and learning ideas are coupled with effective use of ICT to produce deep learning as part of the vision for the school. Chris talks about his vision being of schools that are good, improving and inclusive, and where every child can succeed.

All of these views illustrate the deep moral purpose of leadership, which transcends the overly simplistic notion that schools must concentrate all their efforts in securing high examination results. Examination results are an outcome of an environment that nurtures, respects and develops the individual.

Turning to the leaders' vision for schools in general in the future, Kay refers to schools of the future acting as *'one-stop-shops'* and being the centre of the community, open all hours and being purpose-built for the community.

Chris feels that the quality of primary education is particularly impressive but that work needs to be done on the primary-to-secondary transition in the future. Theresa feels that schools have already radically transformed in recent years, and that looking out beyond the school will be an important way in which schools can seek to constantly improve. Janet reflects how it is perhaps not a good idea to give a general answer for everyone concerning the vision of schools for the future (and this is in itself is perhaps a strong vision). What is right for one school may not be the appropriate solution for another.

The particular circumstances of the school and its community must be considered. Phil supports Janet's thoughts and speaks strongly about the need for *'independence and diversity'* in education.

Derek feels that this is a challenging time for schools and that schools will become *'hubs of learning'* and will often operate in a brokerage role, helping pupils to uncover the kind of education programme that is right for them, both within the school and beyond. Derek's views, like Theresa's above, again hint at the *'personalized learning'* that has recently become a major national discussion point.

Helen talks about schools becoming more and more self-evaluating, and Mike says schools need to be more exciting places with a concentration on entrepreneurial and enterprise skills becoming more the normal experience of pupils, within a greater European framework. Mike feels that schools need to be freer to provide a valuable educational experience for the pupils.

David warns of the danger of technology leading us to a period of *'lack of humanity'*. He argues that personal contact is a vital part of the educational experience of pupils.

Concerning the creation of the vision, involving other people in this and revisiting the vision, Iain says that it is important to speak to all of the stakeholders when creating the vision for the school, and Theresa mentions the key people in her life who have helped her to form her vision for schools. David mentions that it is important for people in the school to know where the school is at in order for the vision to be created, which supports the views of MacGilchrist (referred to on page 14), who talks about a leader's ability to take a holistic view of the organization, including its journey to the current reality. David also says that although visions are wonderful, they are probably always unachievable – which this time supports Kakabadse's view, stated above, that 'for some, vision is that perfect state that might never be reached, but which one never stops trying to achieve'. The same is expressed in a different way by Susan, above.

Eddie tells how his vision for education has come from his own personal experience, which is in agreement with the view also expressed by Theresa, who herself adds that self-evaluation is an important part of forming the vision of the school.

'Whatever the reason, our continued habit of linking leadership with position signals our inability to grasp how organizations are changing.'

Sally Helgesen

Distributed leadership

This section concerns the following:

1.2.1 **What distributed leadership means for all of us**

> ‣ Nurturing individuals nurtures the organization

1.2.2 **The challenge**

> ‣ The softer things are harder

1.2.3 **Indirect leadership**

> ‣ Another view of what it means

1.2.4 **Emergent leaders**

> ‣ Growing leaders

1.2.5 **From controlling events to controlling probabilities and organizational intelligence**

> ‣ Opening up the possibilities for development

1.2.6 Finally, the section looks at the responses of the leaders to the questions on distributed leadership, which include:

Questions on distributed leadership

a) How often do you distribute leadership in the school?
b) Is this done formally or informally?
c) How do you develop leadership in others?
d) How do you see the future of the school in terms of developing distributed leadership?
e) What challenges do we meet in developing leadership at all levels?
f) How do you reconcile being the ultimate leader in your school with growing leadership in others?

1.2.1 What distributed leadership means for all of us

In Section Five of this book Mike Hughes writes around the idea of shared leadership. Mike explains that for him 'shared leadership' rather than 'distributed leadership' better describes the way in which leadership is taken on by a range of people, if not everyone, in an organization. For the purposes of this chapter, however, I will use the term 'distributed leadership'.

The demands now placed on schools are such that the notion of one person being the sole leader is no longer feasible. Nor was this ever the case, of course. There has always been a range of people in any organization, and certainly in schools, who have operated as leaders. Every teacher is a leader in their classroom, for example, but the variety of ways in which people lead in schools is enormous. What is now perhaps different is that the art and science of leadership at all levels is spoken about far more. The NCSL (National College of School Leadership), for example, now have a 'Leading from the middle' programme designed for middle managers in schools, which complements the more established programmes for prospective and serving headteachers and leaders such as NPQH (National Professional Qualification for Headteachers) and HIP (Headteachers' Induction Programme). Many people now argue that the role of a headteacher is to nurture and develop the staff they work with to be effective leaders. The Networked Learning Communities programme operated through the NCSL also has a strong emphasis on distributed leadership as one of its key features. Fullan (2001) speaks directly to headteachers when he says:

> *Ultimately, your leadership in a culture of change will be judged as effective not by who you are as a leader but by what leadership you produce in others.*

1.2.2 The challenge

This notion of distributed leadership presents a real challenge for headteachers. The idea of the charismatic leader is no longer in great favour with most people today. The softer (but more subtle and complex) skill of developing the people a headteacher works with to take on ever more prominent leadership roles requires a very different approach. Fundamental beliefs about leadership being necessarily associated with the traditional hierarchical positions in the school may no longer be the way schools operate in the future. Already there are new pathways that people can take in order to adopt major roles that impact on the development of schools, one example of which is teachers becoming ASTs (advanced skills teachers). A number of schools now have *innovation groups*, made up of staff and sometimes pupils at various stages of their careers, that operate in parallel with the management and leadership structures and can themselves have a real influence on how the school develops. The picture of leadership in schools in the future need not necessarily be a more complex composite than it is now, but it most certainly will be different. Bridges (in Hesselbein et al. 1996) has discussed the way in which successful organizations can break away from leadership based on position. He says:

> 'A traditional organization is hung upon a skeletal system of position-based leaders. De-jobbed organizations, on the other hand, are patterned like an energy field, and leaders function as energy nodes around which activity clusters.'

This description reminds me of a crystal structure or a fractal snowflake with ever repeated patterns. A leader needs to be a catalyst or a nucleus that is responsible for ever-repeating patterns within the organizational structure. As in a crystal structure, there will be strength and reliability, with each person having a distinctive identity but in addition supporting, through critical networks, the bonds that connect to construct the whole. Within the structure there can be discrete units in which individuals cluster to form working groups (these could be departments, or more loosely associated informal partnerships, for example), and these clusters then bond to each other to provide the richness of the organization. When it functions well it is both natural and coherent.

A leader can bring a clear pattern, coherence and structure to a system.

Helgesen (in Hesselbein et al. 1996) supports this view and expresses concern over the way in which certain organizations may be finding it difficult to break away from the structures of the past.

> 'Whatever the reason, our continued habit of linking leadership with position signals our inability to grasp how organizations are changing...
>
> And as grass-roots leadership becomes more common, we will begin to recognize as well led the organizations that are most adept at nourishing leadership independent of official rank or status.'

Entrenched beliefs coupled with established customs and practices can make change something hard for many to take, even when the alternative offers greater rewards both for them personally and for the organization as a whole. The challenge, therefore, of moving over to this new way of viewing leadership in schools is not an easy one. Many of us are stuck with our old perceptions of leadership being in the possession of certain people in structural positions of 'responsibility'. The challenge for the headteacher is to provide the opportunities that allow each individual in a school to contribute, through their own skills, expertise and leadership, to the collective good of the school. People will then take greater ownership, responsibility and pride in the way the school is learning, changing and developing.

1.2.3 Indirect leadership

Pinchot (in Hesselbein et al. 1996) gives another term that may perhaps be used to describe distributed leadership, calling the process 'indirect leadership'. Through indirect leadership senior leaders focus on the vision of the organization, on inspiring values, on listening to and caring for others and leading by personal example. This leaves the way open for others to take on leadership roles themselves, and Pinchot says:

'When indirect leadership is at its best, the people say, "We did it ourselves." The more indirect the method of leadership, the more room there is for other leaders within the organization.'

Providing the right climate for leadership at all levels is not an easy task, but it is a key role of the headteacher. When the appropriate ethos is established and everyone in the community is valued, then people will have the courage and confidence to take on leadership that can truly advance a school. Pinchot, again, says:

'Effective leaders today use the tools of community building to create an environment in which many leaders can emerge.'

For the innovation that the education system needs to take place, the potential that is found rooted in each individual must be released. More leaders are needed and more leaders need to be developed to engage with and adapt to the changing world and the changing education system that we must provide. All employees must be encouraged to have the confidence to take their turn in leadership – to play their part. The danger is that without this, people will simply do what they are told without feeling part of the great advancement that is possible – in other words, they will not feel committed to moving the school from something that is 'good' to something 'great'. Peter Senge (in Hessebein et al. 1996) says that:

'Hierarchical authority, as it has been used traditionally in Western management, tends to evoke compliance, not foster commitment.'

We need innovation in education, and this will be achieved when more people feel ownership through their personal leadership – both within schools and more broadly within the education system that serves the needs of our pupils.

1.2.4 Emergent leaders

One of the challenges in identifying and instating leadership in others is that different people will be needed to take the lead at different times, depending on what is required. Emergent leaders will need to be allowed to step forth and offer their particular skills and expertise on an ongoing basis. A leader will therefore need to be on the lookout, constantly monitoring staff in the school and seeking out ways in which they can contribute to the shared vision that the school has. In ever growing, more complex organizations the traditional leaders can only intervene in given, selected situations, and therefore they carry a smaller percentage of the total given load. Senge (in Hesselbein et al. 1996) adds that:

'Appointed leaders will not play the key leadership roles but will be perpetual diagnosticians who will be able to empower different people at different times and to let emergent leadership flourish.'

Leaders of schools will need to realize that enabling and empowering others is the real measure of their leadership. By apparently giving away control and leadership, their influence and leadership can in fact grow. It is through others that they display real leadership – a leadership contributing towards a collective vision. Titles are of no importance in terms of where leadership ideas may emerge to advance a school. In fact, those with the traditional higher positions in the hierarchical framework should view themselves as servants to those they are seeking to empower with leadership. Pollard (in Hesselbein et al. 1996) expresses this as follows:

'Because leaders make things happen through others, they must be generous in their delegation of authority and responsibility.'

and

'Servant leaders are givers, not takers. They never hold on to a position or title. They have the job because they can live without it. This requires all good leaders to have a plan for succession and for the development of future leaders. Servant leaders promote diversity, recognizing that people's differences can strengthen the group.'

An effective leader provides a service – a giver and not a taker.

Leaders in schools also have a responsibility to ensure that the school has capacity to continue to grow, should any individual, including themselves, leave. They must prepare for succession and this is another reason why it is important to distribute leadership and nurture the leaders of the future. Decrane (in Hesselbein et al. 1996) emphasises the leader's key role in developing other leaders within the organization:

'Effective leaders in business, if they are to build their organizations for the long term, must have the capacity to cultivate the next wave of leaders, or their contributions are unlikely to last much longer than their physical presence within the company. Identifying leaders in an organization is challenging.'

The other important thing that an environment that nurtures and breeds leaders brings to an organization is a sense of energy. The energy an organization needs cannot come from one leader. 'The cloak of leadership is heavy and needs to be shared. No one person can lead or energize an organization,' W. H. Plamondon (in Hesselbein et al. 1996) has said. Both this view and the quote from Decrane above emphasise the limitations of the charismatic leader.

1.2.5 From controlling events to controlling probabilities and organizational intelligence

Sergiovanni (2002) talks about how providing leadership opportunities for others, distributing leadership, shifts the role of headteachers from controlling 'events' to controlling 'probabilities'. He argues that with more flexibility, with more freedom, with a greater scope for creativity, people can achieve greater things than what is possible when events are controlled. A leader, then, is controlling the probability of success, but not the events leading to it. And so Sergiovanni says:

Controlling probabilities rather than events may make more sense.

Sergiovanni claims, like other writers already mentioned here, that it is not always easy for leaders in schools, or indeed policy makers, to give up the idea of control over people and events.

On a national level the DfES now talks about a movement from 'informed prescription' to 'informed professionalism', with schools taking ever greater control of their futures. This is represented in the diagram below. There seems to be a growing realization that this is the way that both schools individually and the education system collectively can truly flourish.

The big picture ...

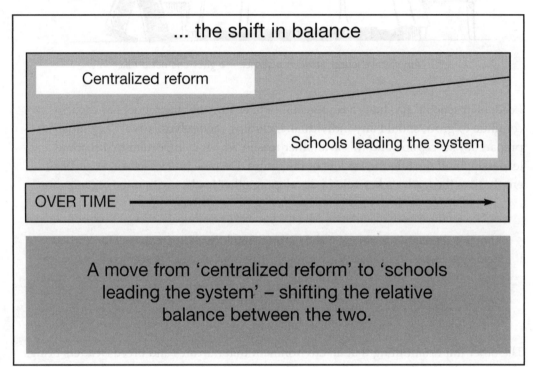

Sergiovanni says that an organization that wants to be free from direct leadership, and therefore more able to develop and embed distributed leadership, needs to establish organizational intelligence. There are five factors (see diagram opposite) which combine in producing organizational intelligence, and these are for schools to be able to:

▶ perceive

▶ memorize

▶ reason

▶ demonstrate imagination

▶ be motivated.

He also says: 'The more intelligently they behave, the less direct leadership they need from heads.'

Organizational intelligence: the five factors

In schools where there is a high level of organizational intelligence there is the ability to progress without the constant, direct input of the headteacher. Schools with high organizational intelligence can have more distributed, widespread leadership – and conversely, schools with distributed, widespread leadership tend to be more organizationally intelligent. These schools have developed a capacity enabling them to sustain growth and progress.

1.2.6 Distributed leadership – what the leaders filmed for VITAL 3 say

Many writers, including Sergiovanni (see above), have said that leaders must be prepared to stand back and hand out leadership. Eddie clearly agrees with this notion and says: *'I think that real power and real leadership is giving it away.'*

One clear reason why this is essential today is that the leadership of a school is too complex and big an issue to be taken on by one person. Anne, for example says: *'I believe as a head, as a leader, you can't do everything yourself. The trust needs to be there.'*

Kay supports this and says: *'If schools are going to function in a way that meets the needs of the children, there needs to be distributed leadership. A head can't do it all.'*

The importance of trust, mentioned above by Anne, is another recurring theme, and Theresa expresses it this way: *'I think the process of developing leadership in others is based on trust. I think that mutual trust is absolutely at the heart of successful leadership.'*

LEEDS COLLEGE OF BUILDING LIBRARY

Theresa also emphasises that mutual understanding and commitment towards a shared goal is important. This is part of the shared vision that has been nurtured and developed by people in the school. This theme is repeated by Derek who says: *'I think everyone is a leader in the school. We are all singing from the same song-sheet.'*

The way in which everyone in the organization is viewed as a leader is another repeated theme. Kay says: *'Every person at Swiss Cottage is a leader.'*

Chris supports this idea: *'The critical thing is to get people to understand that leadership resides in every single member of the team.'*

Phil adds: *'Every member of staff is a leader, a curriculum leader, a learning leader, a learner themselves.'*

Janet adds: *'I believe that leadership is a shared activity.'*

Mike makes a useful distinction between delegated responsibility and distributed leadership. He says: *'Delegated responsibility is taking charge of something and looking after it. Distributed leadership is actually taking something and leading it so that you have the direction, the steer and the pace.'*

David adds to the understanding that distributed leadership is about more than handing over a task to someone else: *'I don't just delegate the tasks, I delegate the responsibility with it and the responsibility is the leadership bit.'*

David reflects on something that became clear to him during an LPSH (Leadership Programme for Serving Heads) course. He says that he discovered that he had none of the styles of leadership that were being discussed, but adds that *'then I came back and thought about my leadership team and they had virtually all of them between them.'*

David says that he realized that he was responsible for the leadership team and they in fact had all the leadership styles. David's honesty and modesty illustrate two points. First of all, a leader does not need to feel that they have all of the 'qualities, skills and talents' that the organization as a whole requires to be successful. Secondly, David is, through his comments, placing the credit for the success within the school at the door of other people. Jim Collins, in *Good to Great*, talks about this being one of the qualities of the top, 'level-five', leaders.

The honesty and modesty of the leaders is again illustrated through Iain's comments. He says: *'One of the nicest challenges that I meet in developing leadership is when I see them becoming better leaders than I am.'*

A leader must not be afraid to enable people to develop in such a way that they can ultimately exceed the original leader's capacity. This illustrates the strength of leaders. Real leadership is about empowering others.

The role of the students in leadership is mentioned a number of times, including Derek's comment that: *'In terms of distributed leadership the idea of students also being leaders in the school is an important one.'*

David remarks on the additional challenges that distributed leadership can bring for the headteacher, as discussed earlier. He says: *'If one distributes leadership, then one must expect to be challenged.'*

David goes on to say that the challenges can sometimes appear to create anarchy, but adds that: *'I quite enjoy the disarray out of which order will come, because it will be a shared decision.'*

Releasing the energy, creativity and power within people can sometimes feel dangerous, but it is only by doing this that great progress can take place, with people feeling a real sense of pride and ownership in the development of the school. Distributed leadership is about releasing the individual leadership capacities of people, and these might, and hopefully will, be very different from that of the headteacher. Ian says: *'Being a leader is not to encourage lots of followers.'* Followers, as Iain refers to them here, will not provide the variety and alternative perspective that a school needs.

Theresa says that one of the challenges of headship for her is to *'look for the potential for leadership'* in others. This is balanced by the reality that Theresa and everyone observes, and that Mike expresses – that *'not everyone aspires to lead'*. What is critical in the process of distributed leadership is, as Kay says, to be *'very clear about the outcomes we want'*. The outcomes are known because they are part of the shared vision for the school. Kay also says that in practical terms support must be provided at all times if the leadership that is being nurtured is to be successful. Kay adds that: *'We are really into growing people – that is what we live and breath here.'*

Linking with the previous chapter on vision, Derek says: *'I've always felt you can only realize a vision through other people.'*

In order to realize the vision through people beyond the headteacher, every member of the school has to feel part of the leadership process. This is why distributed leadership is so important.

The learning school

This section concerns the following:

1.3.1 **sharing and learning from knowledge**

‣ a combination of explicit and tacit knowledge

1.3.2 **the role model**

‣ modelling learning for others and with others

1.3.3 **learning organizations and learning for all**

‣ the dual role

1.3.4 Finally, the section looks at the responses of the leaders to the following question on the learning school:

Question on the learning school

A number of commentators talk about developing a 'learning school' and the headteacher as the lead learner. What does this mean for you and your school?

1.3.1 Sharing and learning from knowledge

In his book *Leading in a Culture of Change* (2001) Michael Fullan says he believes that the 'average company is as bad as the average school system, when it comes to knowledge sharing' but that 'the best companies are better than the best school systems'. Fullan goes on to state:

> 'It is one of life's great ironies; schools are in the business of teaching and learning, yet they are terrible at learning from each other. If they ever discover how to do this, their future is assured.'

It might seem obvious, but I suppose the question should be asked as to why a school should be bothered about building its knowledge, and why a school can't simply survive on what it has so far? Will this concentration on knowledge-sharing, knowledge-creation and knowledge-management be a thing that is here today and gone tomorrow? The answer is a definite no! The reality is that we are in a world where there is an abundance of knowledge and information to be accessed. But only if we can use this to become better learners, and therefore better schools with better teachers and pupils, who themselves learn more effectively, will the knowledge and information be of any use. We have to make sense of the knowledge and information in order to learn from it. Schools that can do this are in a powerful position.

Writers have distinguished between two types of knowledge. These are:

▸ **explicit knowledge** (words and numbers that can be communicated in the form of data and information)

▸ **tacit knowledge** (skills, beliefs and understanding that are below the level of awareness).

Explicit knowledge is an easier quantity to measure, and as a result has been favoured in our educational system. On the other hand, tacit knowledge is viewed by some as the more important, but because it is highly personal, difficult to formalize and difficult to categorize, it is difficult to communicate and share with others. Knowledge in this respect is being described as very much to do with people – and in fact people are at the core of tacit knowledge. Even subjective insights, intuitions and hunches fall within the category of tacit knowledge. Tacit knowledge is often what makes a person 'tick', impacting on their actions and being a core part of their ideals, values and emotions.

It is also worthwhile here making the distinction between knowledge and information. Knowledge, as distinct from information 'is closely attached to human emotions, aspirations, hopes and intentions' (Von Krogh in Fullan 2001, p. 81). The emphasis on the individual and on humanity in all of this is heart-warming for me, as I suspect it is for you. Von Krogh describes how knowledge-enabling within an organization relies on a deep sense of the emotional knowledge and care in the organization which results in highlighting 'how people treat each other' and 'encourages creativity'. The leader therefore has a significant role to play in the school in terms of developing a knowledge-enabling environment in the school. With knowledge-enabling comes a culture of care 'which is vital for successful performance' (Von Krogh in Fullan 2001. p. 81). The five dimensions of this are shown below.

There may sometimes be the feeling that in order to share knowledge there must first be good relationships, a sense of trust – but this need not necessarily always be the case. Dixon (2000) describes how in Ford plants (existing in a highly competitive world) there is a reliance on exchanging knowledge about best practice in order that they can all improve. Through this exchange of knowledge, relationships grow and trust develops. This is the thought process that schools must employ if they too are to grow and develop. By engaging in knowledge exchange, the culture can change between schools – waiting for a culture to develop before exchanging knowledge may mean it will never happen in certain situations.

1.3.2 The role model

The role that the leader in a school plays in developing a learning culture is critical, and writers have commented on the leader in an organization operating as the lead learner. Senge (1990) says:

'We are coming to believe that leaders are those people who "walk ahead", people who are genuinely committed to deep change in themselves and in their organization. They lead through developing new skills, capabilities and understandings. And they come from many places within an organization.'

The complexity of this learning role among all the other things a leader does is also evident. There are many apparent contradictions that need to be carefully balanced. Schein, in Hesselbein et al. (1996), expresses this as follows.

> 'The leader of the future will be a person … Who can lead and follow, be central and marginal, be hierarchically above and below, be individualistic and a team player, and, above all, be a perpetual learner.'

Covey (in Hesselbein et al. 1996) talks about the effective leader's tacit knowledge (mentioned earlier), their desire to constantly grow through learning, and the way they view change. Covey says:

> 'The leader of the future, of the next millennium, will be one who creates a culture or a value system centred upon principles. Creating such a culture in a business, government, school, hospital, non-profit organization, family, or other organization will be a tremendous and exciting challenge in this new era and will only be achieved by leaders, be they emerging or seasoned, who have the vision, courage, and humility to constantly learn and grow.'

Hesselbein et al. go on to say that those people and organizations who have a passion for learning – learning through listening, seeing emerging trends, sensing and anticipating needs in the marketplace, evaluating past successes and mistakes, and absorbing the lessons that conscience and principles teach us, to mention just a few ways – will have enduring influence. He suggests that such learning leaders will not resist change, but rather they will embrace it.

W. H. Plamondon (in Hesselbein et al. 1996) has, like others, drawn an analogy between an organization and an organic system. Just as an organic system relies on the environment and is in tune with it, so a school as an organization must be constantly aware of the immediate environment and the more distant (some would argue the 'world') environment:

> 'An organization is more than the sum of its people, products, and capital. It's organic. It has a life of its own. If it is to stay healthy and grow, its leaders need to keep it open to the environment and attuned to the signals of the market.'

Stoll (2001) and others have emphasised that not only does an organization like a school need to learn in order to develop, but that its very survival depends on it.

It has been suggested by some that for an organization to survive and develop, the rate of learning within the organization must be equal to, or greater than, the rate of change in the external organization. To be effective, therefore, a school must become a learning organization, namely an organization that learns and an organization that encourages learning in its people.

1.3.3 Learning organizations and learning for all

It may be useful here to draw the distinction between the learning organization and learning for all. First of all, learning organizations have the characteristics shown in the figure opposite. Looking at each of these elements:

> *Treating teachers as professionals.* This accepts that teaching is complex and that nothing about it is uniform. Learning organizations trust teachers to make decisions that benefit children.

> *High-quality staff development.* We must invest in teachers' learning in order to impact on pupil learning. (More is said about this in the section on continuing professional development in Book 2, Section 5.) As Fullan has said, as long as there is the need for improvement – namely, forever – there will be a need for professional development.

> *Encouraging teacher leadership and development.* Successful leaders are leaders of leaders (Barth 1990). This takes us back to the earlier discussion on distributed leadership.

> *Promoting collaboration for improvement.* The rich mix here is that of seeking continuous improvement while respecting that pupils and teachers are all individuals under the umbrella of collaboration.

> *Clear induction procedures.* Welcoming people into the organization to replace those leaving, so that the organization can perpetuate a learning culture.

> *Functioning within a context.* Being aware of the national, regional and local context.

> *Working to change things that matter.* This may seem obvious, but is not always what people concentrate on. It is no good being busy if the endeavour will not develop the school.

> *Sweat the small stuff.* The everyday things that teachers, parents, the school community all take to heart have all to be considered in a learning organization. These include things that staff, pupils and parents must all trust in. So discipline, routines, decision making, conflict resolution, communications and public relations must all be dealt with in such a way that they don't interfere with developmental, curricular, teaching and learning changes. Effective day-to-day administration is essential and can be difficult when the leadership is concentrating on providing guidance for continuous school improvement. Sergiovanni (2002) says, 'This combination of moving forward while maintaining stability can make the job at times seem daunting.'

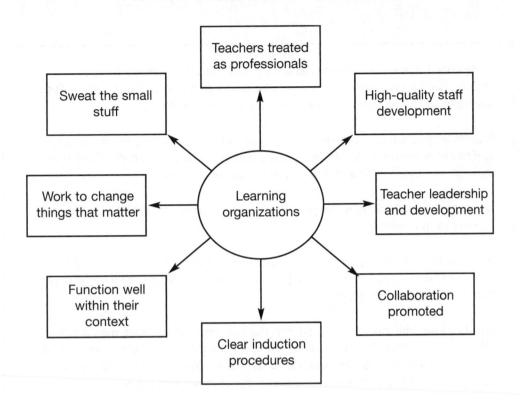

Within the structure of a learning school it is important to encourage each individual to be a learner as well. As long ago as 1993 the National Commission said that 'everyone must want to learn and have ample opportunity and encouragement to do so'.

It is therefore important that all school partners should continue to want to learn; in doing so they set role models for pupils in the school. In addition a number of writers (Stoll included) have said that a crucial contributor to pupil learning is teacher learning. Barth (1990) argues that

'... probably nothing in a school has more impact on students in terms of skills development, self-confidence, or classroom behaviour than the personal and professional growth of their teachers.'

In a learning organization the continuing development of teachers and all adults is an essential prerequisite. MacBeath has said that 'the more we peel back the layers of effective, and less effective, schools, the closer we get to the core of what makes a school work – a commitment to, and joy in, learning'. This applies to the learning of adults in the school as much as it does for pupils.

1.3.4 The learning school – what the leaders say

As described above, a school needs an open ethos in order to become a learning organization. This is expressed by Eddie, who says: *'I believe it is about culture. About developing a culture that sees learning as a valuable activity.'*

Schools are in a period of continual change, and without a desire to learn, a school will start to wither and die. Helen describes this as follows: *'It is said that if a shark stops moving, it will die. I believe the same can be said of a school.'*

Kay talks about the culture within the school as being one where *'everybody here sees themselves as a learner'.*

If you are learning, then there has to be acceptance that you don't know, and will never reach the state of knowing, all you need to know. Janet says: *'As a school we all agree that we don't know everything.'*

David concurs with this comment and adds that learning is about taking risks at times: *'There is a lot of talk these days about the head being the lead learner. And I think that also goes along with the head being someone who can make mistakes and admit them. I actually think that learning is about making mistakes.'*

Again, Theresa expresses a similar sentiment in a slightly different way: *'We've spent a lot of time over the past two to three years looking at how we learn. I've never stopped learning. It's a humbling experience to sometimes admit that sometimes you don't know all the answers. I think you're a stronger headteacher if you can sometimes say "I don't know how we are going to do that".'*

Chris talks about developing people within the learning context: *'How do you build leadership through the organization, how do you build consistent messages? You've got to develop people; people are your most valuable resource.'*

The emphasis on continuing professional development and learning is again mentioned by Iain, who says the school *'[has] put a massive investment into professional development'.*

Modelling in schools is vitally important. Learning is the key purpose of any school, and modelling learning in every aspect, including the vital elements of social, cultural, vocational and life skills, as well as the more academic aspects, is what a school should encourage in everyone. Phil takes this one step further. In talking about leadership, he says: *'Unless you are a learner, you cannot lead.'*

'*Effective leaders today use the tools of community building to create an environment in which many leaders can emerge.*'

Gifford Pinchot

The role of vision
by Adrian Raynor

This section concerns the following:

1.4.1 Meta, macro and micro

▸ Visionary, strategic and operational

1.4.2 What is vision?

▸ It matters deeply.

1.4.3 The focus of the vision

▸ It needs to be clear.

1.4.4 Sources of vision

▸ It can come from many places.

1.4.5 Visionary thinking

▸ Serial, associative and spiritual intelligence

1.4.6 Conclusion

1.4.1 Meta, macro and micro

Effective leadership in schools is complex and operates at several levels – the visionary, the strategic and the operational. The visionary level is concerned with establishing a direction for the school, and includes creating a vision that will engage people, cohere with their values and beliefs and give a sense of purpose. The strategic level involves the skills of good planning in deciding how to move towards the vision, and building an appropriate culture. At the operational level, it is about leading and managing the various tasks that comprise the strategy at a day-to-day level.

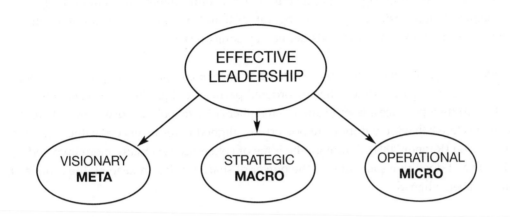

Nichols (1987) called these three levels 'meta, macro and micro' leadership. Meta-leadership is about leading other leaders through a sense of vision and mission. This is an important factor in schools as we move much more towards a model of shared or distributed leadership (for example, Gronn 2000), where leadership is expected at all levels in a school. In this section I shall try to examine what the heads in the video have to say about the visions they embrace, how they develop them, and to consider some of the qualities heads need to operate 'meta-leadership'.

1.4.2 What is vision?

It is only in the last 10 to 15 years that the expectation that a head should have a vision has really developed. This seems surprising when we come to think that a vision is 'a picture of the future we want to create' (Senge 1990). It seems obvious now that a school leader needs to have a clear idea of where the school should be going, why it should be going there and how it should get there. According to Peter Senge (1990), these three questions relate to the associated 'governing ideas' of the enterprise: its vision, its mission and its core values, and its importance for new learning:

> 'Shared vision is vital for the learning organization because it provides the focus and energy for learning. While adaptive learning is possible without vision, generative learning occurs only when people are striving to accomplish something that matters deeply to them.'

Thus the school needs to know what it seeks to create (its vision), why it seeks to create it (its mission or purpose) and the ways in which it will act according to its deep values. As school improvement moves into a new 'generative' phase, where local creativity is being encouraged, the quote is very apt.

This vision, to be effective, needs to be a shared vision, where all are committed to a similar picture, and 'bound together by a common aspiration' (Senge 1990). Without deep commitment, there may be compliance with the vision but not the drive and excitement that can come from full involvement. The vision, then, acts as a motivator by giving meaning and purpose to people's work. It leads to internal commitment. As Fullan (2001), quoting Argyris, points out, internal commitment comes from doing something that is intrinsically rewarding, rather than from the external commitment shown towards goals and methods defined by someone else.

More recently, influences from the emerging science of complexity support and extend what Senge is saying. Just as when disordered particles of light become ordered (or coherent) they produce a laser beam, the members of a school produce more coherent and effective behaviours if they are powerfully aligned in terms of core values, mission and vision (Raynor 2004). Although the issue of coherence is actually more involved than this, it does give some idea of the power of shared vision in keeping the actions of all members aligned.

A striking feature of the interviews for VITAL 3 is that there is such a variety of values and visions. As one head says, schools have to do what is right for their particular situation: the vision must relate to their children in their community. The variety expressed in the visions reinforces this comment, and makes all the more significant the comment by another head that if there is to be a diverse and responsive education system, then schools must have more independence in order to respond to local needs.

This does not mean, however, that all visions must be 'local' and concerned only with a single school and its students. Some of these heads articulate visions that go beyond individual concerns by relating to the wider system, the purposes of education, the needs of the nation and even beyond.

Fullan (2004) has written that despite our awareness of systems thinking, there seems to be little of it, and in my own book (Raynor 2004) I write about the part that highly developed schools play in creating change in the educational system itself as they respond to the wider relationship of the education process with its environment, and constantly check their own assumptions about educational purposes and provision. This is essentially a matter of seeing the school's role in educating for a better society, as well as focusing on the needs of individual children: it is a wider perception of the whole enterprise.

Looked at in this way, we can begin to understand the varied visions these heads are expressing in terms of where the focus of the vision lies.

1.4.3 The focus of the vision

It is not always easy to see the focus of the vision very precisely, but the heads shown in the video divide roughly into three levels of focus: the individual, the school as an organization, and the wider community. For several of these heads, the focus of the vision lies very much at the level of the individual pupil. Heads spoke of giving a sense of belonging, or creating an environment in which learning could take place, where everyone is a learner reaching their highest potential. Others spoke in similar terms about 'creating expert learners' and providing a wide range of opportunities.

Others added a wider focus on the school itself as an organization. One, for example, stresses the need, as a school, to be at the forefront of initiatives. Another has a vision of the school being at the 'heart of the community', and a local authority provider holds that the school should be 'world-class'. Though he professes to be 'not sure what that means', it is an aspiration, and includes schools being 'good', 'improving', and promoting a 'high achievement culture'.

Just as some heads formulated visions around the school as a unit rather than the individual, others related what the school was trying to achieve with the wider social and economic context. This wider focus was less evident, but was represented by such concerns as 'creating an inclusive society', or being 'at the heart of the community'. However, there was more stress on this aspect when heads were stating their vision for schools in the future, where they spoke of helping to support families at home, or having a 'high moral purpose' to bring the socially disadvantaged to the same level as everyone else so as to ensure a 'better-educated workforce to access world markets'.

The vision of one of the leaders filmed for VITAL 3 effectively linked the levels of individual and community, and spoke of creating 'expert learners' who gain the capacity to be effective citizens and an ensuing capacity within the community. These in turn lead to economic regeneration, and ultimately social regeneration. Again, we see here a vision closely related to the needs of the specific pupils and local situation, and articulated in that way.

How, then, can we explain these different levels of focus? I believe the concept of 'chunking' can be useful here. The idea of chunking comes from the world of computers, and means breaking things down into smaller, or alternatively building them up into larger, pieces. Simply put, ideas can exist in a hierarchy. We are always at some mid-point in a range of values or ideas and can always 'chunk up' by asking 'What is this a part of?' or 'What will this do?' Or we can 'chunk down' by asking 'What is an example of this?' or 'What will be a result of this?' As we chunk up, the concepts tend to become more general or abstract. As we come down the hierarchy, they become more concrete or specific.

Chunking is a very good way to arrive at core values and different levels of vision. Another way is to ask a series of progressive 'why?' questions – for example, 'Why is that important to you?' The figure below is an attempt to show how chunking provides a hierarchy of vision considerations.

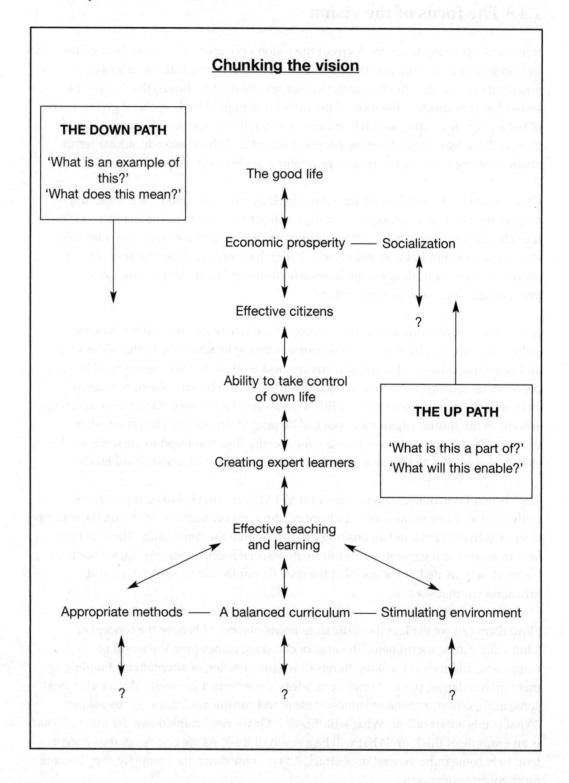

Here I have included some of the statements the heads made into a form of hierarchy, and added a few myself for purposes of illustration. You may well disagree with the position in which I have put some items, but I have tried to show three features of chunking:

1. As you chunk upwards, purposes and visions become more general or abstract, and are therefore capable of an increasing number of interpretations. It is also more difficult to see obviously the practical applications in school.

2. As you chunk downwards, there is an increasingly more precise and actionable focus.

3. Further, as you move down the hierarchy, there tend to be more opportunities to chunk sideways to alternatives, though this applies to all levels to an extent. These alternatives then set up their own hierarchies.

Of course, it is important to realize that the hierarchy I have created here is not the only one: for each school undertaking this exercise there would be a different outcome to reflect that school's individual context. These might, however, tend towards general agreement at the very highest, most abstract levels. I think what is important about this short illustration is that the visions described by the heads fall at various different levels in this hierarchy. There could be several reasons for this, but two are most likely. First, there may be the need to feel the vision is actionable. The higher, more abstract levels are not easy to action without chunking down many levels first. Where the vision is described in a mid-level position, items in the upper part may be left as 'understood' but not articulated. Secondly, there is the possibility that the 'higher level', system-wide vision should be the province of government or LEA, much as one respondent said was once the case. One example might be the way Sir Alec Clegg led the vision for primary schools in the West Riding of Yorkshire.

Since we adopt many processes in schools to attain our outcomes, or products, it is perhaps unsurprising that these also find their place in the chunking hierarchy. In fact, the processes involved in education were more prominent in the stated visions than were the products. These processes were expressed in a variety of ways, such as standards of 'excellence', an exciting environment, a caring school, inclusion, and the like.

In this section I have briefly examined the focus of the stated visions and suggested that there are several 'levels' at which vision can operate, and that visions may incorporate both product and process. The use of the chunking technique could be helpful for schools to think out their vision at several levels. We now turn to the question of where the vision comes from.

1.4.4 Sources of vision

Heads said the visions they articulated came from a variety of sources. For some, a key source was their own experiences or ideas. An example given by one leader was 'what I would want for my child', while others talked about deeply held convictions stemming from their own education. For some, it was key people in their past – for example, the French teacher 'who made my lessons a complete joy'. For others it was key people in the present, such as staff, governors and children who played a role in modifying their vision. One head, for example, put her vision in place for the first year of her headship and then asked others in the school to consider it, and presumably modify it.

Central initiatives can also contribute to the vision. One head cited the 'Healthy Schools' initiative as a way of structuring their work and checking they are moving in the right direction – for example, it means 'the school has a commitment to the physical, social, emotional and moral welfare of the people in the establishment'. Similarly, the 'Arts Mark' shows the school is working on the creative aspects of the curriculum. While these are, strictly speaking, catalysts for achieving the vision, it would be surprising if there were not some reciprocal action in formulating or modifying it.

Several of the heads stressed the idea that the vision was contextual and might need 'compromise'. As one of them, with 23 of headship experience in different schools, said:

> 'The vision can't be translated from one school to another: it has to fit that school. In creating it, you have to speak to all stakeholders to see what their visions are … because if their visions are not part of your vision, you can't develop your own vision.'

Several of the heads stressed this need to involve all stakeholders in creating the vision. Although some referred to this as a 'compromise', the head quoted above realized a different process was involved. He said he held 'a great discussion on what the school should be achieving' which enabled everyone to understand what they were trying to do – 'otherwise those who sweep the corridors at the end of the day won't understand what we are trying to achieve and won't join in'. This, then, was not a matter of 'compromise'. Rather, from the 'massive dialogue', he would 'let the vision draw itself out'. Complexity theory tells us that multiple factors, like the various values and visions held by a variety of stakeholders, can self-organize and produce an emergent outcome

A leader's vision can act as a 'strange attractor'.

Effective Leadership in Schools

that is not a compromise, but one which transcends and includes all. Elsewhere, I have described the need for the vision to act as a 'strange attractor' (Raynor 2004). In complexity theory, attractors 'draw' actions towards them.

The 'strange attractor' draws the system to different points, but within a fixed range. Thus it can give direction while allowing some variety of outcomes within that range. To function as a strange attractor, the vision needs a certain level of generality (compare the vision hierarchy above) from which all individuals can each construct their meaning – and yet it needs to be sufficiently precise to guide action. Thus it will resonate with all and it will be precise enough, but not too precise. The role of the head is one of facilitator, helping this emergent process to happen but without directing it, and it is clear that securing such agreement from all stakeholders about what important principles and values should inform the running of the school is a central role of headship.

1.4.5 Visionary thinking

Do heads need any kind of special intelligence to generate such effective visions for their school? Based on current brain research, Zohar and Marshall (2000) identify three levels of thinking and intelligence.

At one level there is *serial thinking*. This is linear and logical thinking – the type of thinking that IQ is based on, derived from logic. It is rational thinking, and we use it a lot in practical day-to-day life. It is reasonably precise and accurate, but tends to work in straight lines from A to B and doesn't like ambiguity.

Associative thinking works differently, helping us to form associations between things, and operates in the brain, not serially, but through neural networks. At its simplest, this is the process Pavlov's dogs went through. As such, it is experience-based, trial-and-error learning and is used in skill development, and is a fundamental way emotions are built up. At a higher level, it plays a big role in pattern recognition. Zohar and Marshall refer to this capacity as EQ, or emotional intelligence, perhaps in a wider sense than Goleman (1996).

The third level they call *spiritual intelligence* (SQ), and they define it as '[the] intelligence with which we have access to deep meaning, fundamental values and a sense of abiding purpose in our lives ... it allows us to see the larger context in which events take place and to see the big picture. It gives our lives an overarching canopy of meaning and value' (Zohar and Marshall 2004).

SQ goes beyond the other two forms of intelligence, addressing meaning and giving us a sense of unity in looking at a situation. This unitive thinking helps us to grasp the full surrounding context of a situation, and is a basis for exploring meaning and transformation.

A leader's intelligence is a rich, blended cocktail.

It seems to me that meaning and transformation are at the heart of the visionary process, and if so, we need to develop this aspect of our intelligence to make sense of the future world that our education must support and of the transformations that may be necessary to prepare young people for it. It is about being holistic, and for this reason, in formulating visions, we have to have a sense of how everything fits together – the unitive aspect of thinking. This in turn means not only having some view of the future world, but how our children can be empowered to affect it positively. It is SQ that helps us to discover new values as well as recognize our current ones: it is the 'guide from within' that helps us to found our actions on deep principles.

Fullan has explored similar territory in his recognition of moral purpose as a key force in change in complex times. By moral purpose, he means 'acting with the intention of making a positive difference in the lives of employees, customers and society as a whole' (Fullan 2001), a sentiment referred to in almost the same words by one of the heads. Moral purpose embraces aspects of ends – for example, improving life and how we live together – and the processes by which we pursue those ends. As he says, 'you simply cannot be effective without behaving in a morally purposeful way' (Fullan 2001). Even governments are being called upon to have visions that go beyond a concern for economic prosperity. Recently, the chairman of the Sustainable Development Commission complained that the British government's central objective remained as conventional economic growth rather than the well-being of society and the planet as a whole, and that the definition of economic growth should be revised to take account of environmental effects (*The Independent*, 13 April 2004).

1.4.6 Conclusion

In this section we have looked at the importance of vision in education and the focus of the visions these heads expressed. We have looked at the way visions are formed and considered the thinking qualities that are needed for this. In conclusion I would like once again to consider the relationship of single school visions to the wider system.

While all the heads expressed deep commitments, it was noticeable that, apart from one head who referred to the need for a better-educated workforce 'to access world markets', there was little or no explicit mention of the future world that students will experience, or of the kinds of qualities and skills they will need. Even some of the generally accepted needs such as adaptability, tolerance of change, flexible attitudes and the ability to constantly re-skill are scarcely mentioned. Perhaps these are now such a part of the conventional wisdom that they were taken for granted. Or could it be that heads accept the centrally directed curriculum, and then concentrate on 'excellence' in provision, leaving the philosophy to others? Or perhaps they restricted their answers, since the question asked about vision for their school.

This begs the question of whether a school's vision can exist at a lower level on the 'vision hierarchy' without at least taking into account and being aware of these wider features of world trends. Talking about sustainability, Fullan (2004) is clear that we need to train leaders to think in wider terms of the system as a whole. He calls such leaders 'the new theoreticians'. Hargreaves (2003) has written about the value of networks in disseminating change laterally, and I have written about schools co-evolving (Raynor 2002). For these processes to work effectively in the pursuit of educational change, the sense of vision needs to incorporate future needs and outcomes for the individual, the community and, increasingly, the world, if education is going to 'make a difference'.

References

Fullan M. (2001) *Leading in a Culture of Change*. San Francisco: Jossey-Bass.

Fullan M. (2004) *Leadership and Sustainability*. University of Toronto. Paper prepared for Hot Seat, Urban Leadership Community, England (March).

Goleman D. (1996) *Emotional Intelligence: Why it can matter more than IQ*. London: Bloomsbury.

Gronn P. (2000) 'Distributed properties: a new architecture of leadership.' *Educational Management and Administration* 28 (3), 317–338.

Hargreaves D. H. (2003) *Education Epidemic*. London: Demos.

Nichols, J. (1987) 'Leadership in organizations: Meta, macro and micro.' *European Management Journal* 6, 16–25.

Raynor A. (2002) 'Complexity, creativity and personal development in headship.' In Trorey G. and Cullingford C. *Professional Development and Institutional Needs*. Aldershot: Ashgate.

Raynor A. (2004) *Individual Schools, Unique Solutions*. London: RoutledgeFalmer.

Senge P. (1990) *The Fifth Discipline: The art and practice of the learning organization*. New York: Doubleday. (Reprinted in the UK 1999. London: Random House.)

Zohar D. and Marshall I. (2000) *Spiritual Intelligence: The ultimate intelligence*. London: Bloomsbury.

Zohar D. and Marshall I. (2004) *Spiritual Capital: Wealth we can live by*. London: Bloomsbury.

Why share leadership?

by Mike Hughes

This section concerns the following:

1.5.1 Shared leadership – to what extent and why?

▸ Is it important?

1.5.2 Implement, interpret, initiate

▸ How far does shared leadership extend?

1.5.3 Compliance to commitment

▸ Where on the spectrum are you?

1.5.4 Perception and extent of shared leadership

▸ Using the institutional structure diagram

1.5.5 Context

▸ It isn't always the same.

1.5.6 Finally, the section raises a few questions for reflection.

1.5.1 Shared leadership – to what extent and why?

Shared leadership – the concept that leadership resides not with the one or the few but with the many – is currently in fashion. Many are talking about it, advocating it or actually doing it. Even the England rugby team has captains for various aspects of the game – a line-out captain, a captain for defence, and so on, working alongside the team captain. Some may dismiss it as the latest fad and more trendy jargon, while others argue that sharing leadership throughout the institution is not only necessary – the sheer scale and complexity of the contemporary leadership challenge is simply too much for a single head or small leadership team – but desirable: the significance of ownership, commitment and involvement have long been recognized as key ingredients of successful institutions.

This section is neither a justification of, nor an advert for, shared leadership. It has been written, not to provide answers, but to ask questions; questions that, it is hoped, will generate discussion and debate in schools and help senior school leaders reflect on the way in which leadership is interpreted and exercised in their school. It is based around two fundamental questions:

  ‣ To what extent is leadership shared in your school?

  ‣ Why?

The notion of shared leadership is open to considerable interpretation. This means that when two heads claim to share leadership, the practice between the two schools may vary significantly. This is, in part at least, due to the rather simplistic way in which we often talk about shared leadership; you either do it or you don't, you either share it or, presumably, keep it to yourself. It may be more helpful to consider not just whether we share leadership or not, but the *extent* to which leadership is shared and embedded across a school.

It is also apparent that when people talk about shared leadership they often mean delegated management. There is a fundamental difference between the two. It is the reason why many prefer the phrase 'shared leadership' to 'distributed leadership'. Distributed or delegated leadership implies a hierarchical model, in that leadership is someone's to distribute. Shared leadership is a different concept altogether.

Similarly, we have to be clear about the difference between leadership and management. Delegating or distributing management tasks to individuals or groups is not the same thing as sharing leadership. This is not about semantics; it is a *fundamental* distinction.

  ‣ Do you share or delegate leadership?

  ‣ Are you sharing/delegating leadership or management?

1.5.2 Implement, interpret, initiate

The extent to which leadership is genuinely being shared across an institution can be gauged using the '3 i's' model. It is not the definitive guide but may be a helpful rule of thumb.

When we say that leadership is shared and that X has a leadership role to play, what do we mean? (X could be an individual or a team of teachers. Teams can be semi-permanent – for example, a department or year team, or may have come together for a specific purpose.) Does X (the individual or team) have responsibility to simply *implement*? Are they able to *interpret*? Or do they have authority to *initiate*?

Implement

This is the level at which staff are required to implement policies and decisions that have been made by someone else – the 'someone else' being higher up the hierarchy.

It applies at a number of levels: senior staff are required to implement decisions that have been taken by the head. Middle leaders are required to implement policies that have been made by the senior leadership team. Teachers are required to implement policies that have been made by middle/senior leaders.

At this level, people have responsibility without authority. Their role is to follow in a direction that has been set for them. It is clearly an autocratic, hierarchical leadership model.

Interpret

At this level teachers are able to interpret policies and operate within a looser framework, such that departments are able to interpret school policy, and/or teachers are able to interpret departmental policy.

In many respects there is a considerable blurring in this stage. People certainly have increased flexibility – but whether they have genuine freedom to lead is less certain. They certainly have responsibility, but significantly less authority. The broad direction has already been set.

Initiate

At this level, individuals and teams not only have responsibility, they have significant amounts of authority, indeed autonomy, to act and initiate. Although they work towards the shared vision of the institution within the framework that has been collectively agreed, they have considerable freedom to generate policy. They are able to take the school in a new direction.

This model does not imply that 'initiate' is the correct or best stage. Context clearly plays a part in determining leadership style (see page 53). Indeed, it may be appropriate to adopt a different approach with different individuals and teams, or even different schools. So, for example, the history department may be ready to initiate, but the science department, due to a combination of circumstances and personnel, is still at 'interpret'.

1.5.3 Compliance to commitment

Peter Senge and John West-Burnham argue that leadership involves moving people from compliance to commitment. There are some parallels with the 3 i's model. Certainly 'compliance' and 'implement' sit well together and so, it can be argued, do 'commitment' and 'initiate'. Both compliance–commitment and implement–initiate imply a continuum and a sense of evolution. Both pose some interesting questions:

- Do you have to have compliance before you can win commitment?
- Does commitment imply involvement, and therefore shared leadership?
- Do people have to implement before they can be allowed to initiate?
- Where are you, as a school, along this continuum?
- Why? Is the leadership style in your school appropriate for the context?

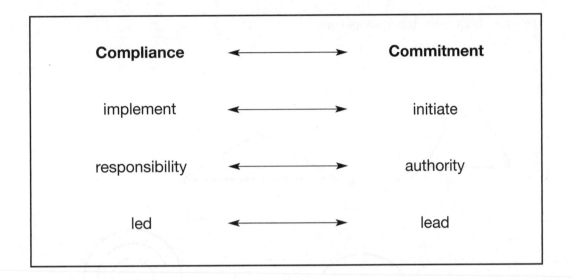

1.5.4 Perception and extent of shared leadership

A commitment by the headteacher to shared leadership is, of course, a significant starting point. However, at least two other factors affect the extent to which leadership is shared and the extent to which this sharing proves effective:

- the perceptions of the staff
- the extent to which leadership is shared by all staff.

Perception

There is no reality as such. There is only perceived reality.

This lovely quote from Tom Peters and Nancy Austin's book *A Passion for Excellence* (Harper Collins 1985) reminds us that perception is everything. Headteachers may claim that leadership is shared throughout the school but the staff often see things very differently. (This very much relates to what Mike says here in the VITAL 3 interviews.)

Extent

There are headteachers who are committed to sharing leadership. However, when this commitment isn't matched by a similar commitment made by the rest of the leadership team or, more usually, middle managers, the laudable intentions of the headteacher are not met, and we could end up with a school that operates as a democratic society based on the principles of shared leadership, and a maths department that is run as a dictatorship.

The following exercise may shed some light on the two points raised above:

1. Draw an 'institutional structure diagram' for your school, showing headteacher, senior team, middle leaders, classroom teachers, and so on.

2. Invite your colleagues to complete the same exercise. Compare the shape of your diagram with those of other people. Are they the same shape?

The most frequently drawn shapes are:

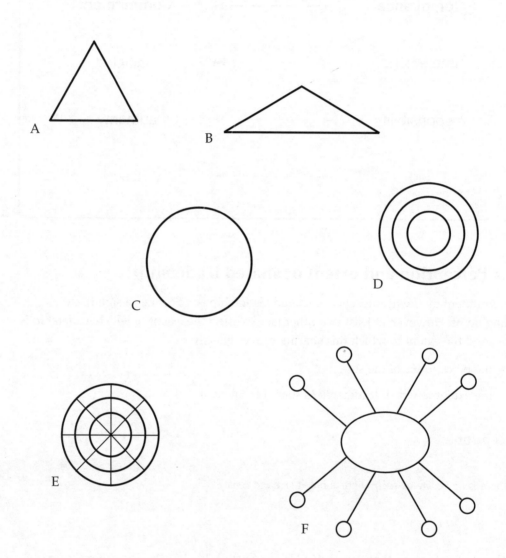

Testing perception

Headteachers are more likely to draw shapes C, D, E or F. However, irrespective of the shape drawn by the head, the teachers in the same school invariably draw a triangle (A or B).

Perceptions are powerful, and based on the individual interpretation of small and subtle messages. For example, many schools have photographs of the teaching staff on display in the entrance hall. Often they are displayed in a triangular layout!

Effective Leadership in Schools

How far does shared leadership extend?

It is not uncommon for headteachers to draw the spider institutional structure diagram (shown below). This is a model based upon high performance teams.

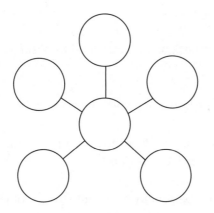

However, the key here is not the overall shape of the diagram, but the shape of the individual teams. Are they circles or triangles? A triangle at the end of the line – which may be reality or perception – may indicate that leadership is being shared from the head and senior team but is not being shared by middle leaders.

1.5.5 Context

Context often plays a role in determining, or at least influencing, leadership style. Many would argue that a struggling school, a school in special measures or a school with high staff turnover, requires a different leadership approach than a high-flying, stable and successful school. Indeed, many would argue that a key to being a successful leader is the ability to adopt a leadership style that is suitable for the particular circumstances.

Context is frequently cited as a barrier to sharing leadership to any significant degree. In schools and situations where there is a need for decisive and significant improvements and for those improvements to be made quickly, many people argue that what is required is firm direction, leadership from the top and compliance from the rest of the staff. 'We're not in a position for sharing leadership' or 'The staff aren't ready for it' are not uncommon views.

Although the logic of this argument is crystal clear, it should be acknowledged that not everyone responds to a particular context in the same way. Although many argue that a struggling school in difficult circumstances, with poor staff morale and so on, demands a tightly controlled, lead-from-the-front approach to headship, not everyone does. There are headteachers who have inherited such schools and have sought to share leadership from day one, seeking to win commitment rather than gain compliance. It simply reminds us that there is always more than one way of achieving an end, and there are as many different leadership styles as there are leaders. For leadership style is not simply a derivative of context. Context may influence style, but so do the beliefs, experiences and personal characteristics of the leader.

LEEDS COLLEGE OF BUILDING
LIBRARY

Which is more powerful: the place or the person? It is often claimed that reluctance to share leadership is an appropriate response to circumstances. There may be an element of truth in that. However, it is worth asking the question: to what extent is it due to the leader feeling personally uncomfortable with the concept?

1.5.6 Finally

The following questions are designed to offer food for thought and prompt discussion, debate and reflection.

1. To what extent is your leadership style determined by context?

2. How does your perception of the context compare with those of other people – including objective outsiders?

3. To what extent do you personally contribute to the context?

4. How will you know when the context has changed sufficiently for you to change your leadership style? What will be the 'triggers'?

5. What will change first: the context (and then you will adapt your leadership style) or your leadership style (which will then influence the context)?

6. To what extent will first impressions make a lasting impression? (For example: you are being authoritarian because of the context. Although you subsequently change your style, is there a danger that the staff will still see you as authoritarian?)

7. Do the staff see your leadership style in the same way as you do? How do you know?

8. Do the staff see your leadership style as a response to context? How do you know?

9. Would another leader working in your school adopt the same style as you? How do you know?

BIBLIOGRAPHY

Barth R. (1990) *Improving Schools from Within. Parents and principals can make a difference.* San Francisco: Jossey-Bass.

Bolam R. (1993) *Recent Developments and Emerging Issues in the Continuing Professional Development of Teachers.* London: GTC.

Collins J. (2002) *Good to Great.* London: Random House.

Cordingley P., Bell M., Rundell B., Evans D. and Curtis A. (2003) 'The impact of collaborative CPD on classroom teaching and learning.' http://eppi.ioe.ac.uk/EPPIweb/home.aspx

Day C. (1999) *Developing Teachers: The challenge of lifelong learning.* London: Falmer.

Day C., Harris A., Hadfield M., Tolley H. and Beresford J. (2003) *Leading Schools in Times of Change.* Maidenhead: Open University Press.

Dixon N. (2000). *Building a New Structure for School Leadership.* Boston: Harvard Business School Press.

Early P. and Bubb S. (2004) *Leading and Managing Continuing Professional Development.* London: Paul Chapman Publishing.

EPPI-Centre. *How does collaborative Continuing Professional Development (CPD) for teachers of the 5-16 age range affect teaching and learning?*

Fullan M. (2001) *Leading in a Culture of Change.* San Francisco: Jossey-Bass.

Hargreaves D. H. (2003) *Education Epidemic.* London: Demos.

Hesselbein F., Goldsmith M. and Beckhard R. (eds) (1996) *The Leader of the Future.* New York: Jossey-Bass.

Kakabadse A., Nortier F. and Abramovici N.-B. (1998) *Success in Sight: Visioning.* London: International Thomson Business Press.

Leithwood K., Jantzi D. and Steinbach R. (2002) *Changing Leadership for Changing Times.* Maidenhead: Open University Press.

MacBeath J. and Mortimore P. (2001) *Improving School Effectiveness.* Maidenhead: Open University Press.

Schleicher, A. (2003) 'Quality and Equity. Benchmarking the Performance of Education Systems.' Presentation at DfES research conference in England.

Senge P. (1990) *The Fifth Discipline.* Reprinted 1999. London: Random House.

Senge P. (2003) *Schools that Learn.* London: Nicholas Brearley.

Sergiovanni T. J. (2002) *Leadership. What's in it for Schools*? London: RoutledgeFalmer.

Stoll L. and Fink D. (2001) *Changing Our Schools.* Maidenhead: Open University Press.

Swainston T. (2002) *Effective Teachers: A reflective resource for enhancing practice.* Stafford: Network Educational Press.

Swainston T. (2003) *Effective Teachers in Primary Schools: A reflective resource for enhancing practice.* Stafford: Network Educational Press.

Index

Other titles from Network Educational Press

ACCELERATED LEARNING SERIES
Accelerated Learning: A User's Guide
    by Alistair Smith, Mark Lovatt & Derek Wise
Accelerated Learning in the Classroom by Alistair Smith
Accelerated Learning in Practice by Alistair Smith
The ALPS Approach: Accelerated Learning in Primary Schools
    by Alistair Smith & Nicola Call
The ALPS Approach Resource Book by Alistair Smith & Nicola Call
ALPS StoryMaker by Stephen Bowkett
MapWise by Oliver Caviglioli & Ian Harris
Creating an Accelerated Learning School by Mark Lovatt & Derek Wise
Thinking for Learning by Mel Rockett & Simon Percival
Reaching out to all learners by Cheshire LEA
Move It: Physical movement and learning by Alistair Smith
Coaching Solutions by Will Thomas & Alistair Smith

ABLE AND TALENTED CHILDREN COLLECTION
Effective Provision for Able and Talented Children by Barry Teare
Effective Resources for Able and Talented Children by Barry Teare
More Effective Resources for Able and Talented Children by Barry Teare
Challenging Resources for Able and Talented Children by Barry Teare
Enrichment Activities for Able and Talented Children by Barry Teare
Parents' and Carers' Guide for Able and Talented Children by Barry Teare

LEARNING TO LEARN
Let's Learn How to Learn: Workshops for Key Stage 2 by UFA National Team
Brain Friendly Revision by UFA National Team
Creating a Learning to Learn School by Toby Greany & Jill Rodd
Teaching Pupils How to Learn by Bill Lucas, Toby Greany, Jill Rodd & Ray Wicks

PRIMARY RESOURCES
*Promoting Children's Well-Being in the Primary Years: The Right from
    the Start Handbook edited* by Andrew Burrell and Jeni Riley
But Why? Developing philosophical thinking in the classroom
    by Sara Stanley with Steve Bowkett
Foundations of Literacy by Sue Palmer & Ros Bayley
Help Your Child To Succeed by Bill Lucas & Alistair Smith
Help Your Child To Succeed – Toolkit by Bill Lucas & Alistair Smith
That's English! by Tim Harding
That's Maths! by Tim Harding
That's Science! by Tim Harding
The Thinking Child by Nicola Call with Sally Featherstone

The Thinking Child Resource Book by Nicola Call with Sally Featherstone
Numeracy Activities Key Stage 2 by Afzal Ahmed & Honor Williams
Numeracy Activities Key Stage 3 by Afzal Ahmed, Honor Williams
       & George Wickham

EXCITING ICT

New Tools for Learning: Accelerated Learning meets ICT by John Davitt
Exciting ICT in Maths by Alison Clark-Jeavons
Exciting ICT in English by Tony Archdeacon
Exciting ICT in History by Ben Walsh

CREATIVE THINKING

Think it–Map it! by Ian Harris & Oliver Caviglioli
Thinking Skills & Eye Q by Oliver Caviglioli, Ian Harris & Bill Tindall
Reaching out to all thinkers by Ian Harris & Oliver Caviglioli
With Drama in Mind by Patrice Baldwin
Imagine That... by Stephen Bowkett
Self-Intelligence by Stephen Bowkett
StoryMaker Catch Pack by Stephen Bowkett

EFFECTIVE LEARNING & LEADERSHIP

Effective Heads of Department by Phil Jones & Nick Sparks
Leading the Learning School by Colin Weatherley
Closing the Learning Gap by Mike Hughes
Strategies for Closing the Learning Gap by Mike Hughes with Andy Vass
Transforming Teaching & Learning
       by Colin Weatherley with Bruce Bonney, John Kerr & Jo Morrison
Effective Learning Activities by Chris Dickinson
Tweak to Transform by Mike Hughes
Making Pupil Data Powerful by Maggie Pringle & Tony Cobb
Raising Boys' Achievement by Jon Pickering
Effective Teachers by Tony Swainston
Effective Teachers in Primary Schools by Tony Swainston

EFFECTIVE PERSONNEL MANAGEMENT

*The Well Teacher – management strategies for beating stress, promoting
    staff health & reducing absence* by Maureen Cooper
Managing Challenging People – dealing with staff conduct
    by Maureen Cooper & Bev Curtis
Managing Poor Performance – handling staff capability issues
    by Maureen Cooper & Bev Curtis
Managing Recruitment and Selection – appointing the best staff
    by Maureen Cooper & Bev Curtis
*Managing Allegations Against Staff – personnel and child protection
    issues in schools* by Maureen Cooper & Bev Curtis